TAMING YOUR
INNER MONKEY

Michael Hill

Avid Readers Publishing Group
Lakewood, California

Taming Your Inner Monkey

Avid Readers Publishing Group

http://www.avidreaderspg.com

ISBN-13:978-1-61286-328-3

Printed in the United States

Table of Contents

DEDICATION v

DISCLAIMER vi

ACKNOWLEDGMENT vii

INTRODUCTION ix

CHAPTER 1: THE HUMAN BRAIN 1

CHAPTER 2: INSPIRATION 11

CHAPTER 3: SUFFERING 19

CHAPTER 4: FAITH 25

CHAPTER 5: THE EXISTENCE OF GOD 31

CHAPTER 6: CONQUERING SELF 41

CHAPTER 7: MEDITATION 51

CHAPTER 8: THE POWER OF POSITIVE THINKING 55

CHAPTER 9: COMPASSION 63

CHAPTER 10: NEUROPSYCHOLOGY AND
COMPASSION   67
CHAPTER 11: HATE   77

CHAPTER 12: HANDLING STRESS   81

CHAPTER 13: GIVING YOUR BRAIN VERBAL
COMMANDS   93

CHAPTER 14: TESTING YOUR HAPPINESS 101

EPILOGUE   107

DEDICATION

This book is dedicated to my wife, Lynne, who has been the most positive influence in my adult life. She has always looked at life with a positive constructive attitude and has never failed to impress me with her acute sense of propriety by always being extremely fair and honest in all her dealings with others. She is my best friend and has been the love of my life for over 40 years (one lucky guy).

DISCLAIMER

I don't profess to be a professional nor an expert in the field of understanding the human brain, nor in the fields of psychology and psychiatry for that matter. I am simply presenting my viewpoint based on operating my own brain for over 70 years. It is my hope that my simple down to earth analysis may help others whose brains are similarly wired. My personal belief is that we have more in common than not, except for those with mental illnesses, like psychopaths, sociopaths, schizophrenics, bipolar or border line personality disorders, anxiety and depression.

Acknowledgment

I would like to thank George Dietrich, my best friend since pre-school, for his excellent editing skills and his life long friendship.

I would also like to thank my sister, Pat Hill, for her incredibly caring heart and invaluable input in proof reading the original manuscript.

And a special thanks to Steve Miller for his excellent cover illustrations that creatively portray both the concept of an out of control monkey and the after effects of the taming process.

Lastly but certainly not least I want to give a huge thanks to my very good friend George Jaramillo for his inspiration without which this book would never have been written.

Thanks to all and God Bless

INTRODUCTION

It all started eight years ago on the day that I retired from a 40-year career of helping turn around and growing a number of manufacturing companies. With a formal education in both Business and Operations Research Engineering, which included two master degrees, I spent very little time reading anything other than business and engineering related books during my career. So immediately upon retirement I embarked on a quest to broaden my overall knowledge of how our brain affects our happiness.

I have come to believe that most everyone has common desires and fears, and sometimes a limited control over their negative thoughts, which I refer to as the brain's default setting. This belief is based on how I view the operation of my brain, but also from insights that I have gained from over 40 years of employing and working with thousands of people at eight companies and with a fair amount of reading since retiring eight years ago. It is with this belief that I have attempted to express my point of view on what I believe to be true. I endeavor to offer insight and practical solutions or methods to help deal with life and its challenges. I take a proactive approach for the pursuit of peace and happiness, while keeping in mind that everything in life is relative and must be viewed in that vein.

I am so convinced that my insights might very well be able to help the majority of people who are neither clinically depressed nor suffering from other forms of mental illness that I felt compelled to share my personal struggles and what eventually has worked for me.

CHAPTER 1
THE HUMAN BRAIN

Despite its flaws, it is our brain that dictates our entire life. Essentially our entire life's experience is a product of our brain.

CHAPTER 1

THE HUMAN BRAIN

If you didn't already know from your under-standing of human anatomy, would your brain be able to tell you precisely where it is located? Close your eyes and concentrate really hard. No, your brain doesn't even have a clue. In ancient times it was thought that the brain resided where the heart is because of the heartbeats.

Another limitation of the brain is that it only reacts to physical pain as a safeguard from hurting ourselves further. It completely ignores mental pain or suffering which can cause great emotional harm.

Our brain also has a bad habit of keeping us from concentrating on just one thing at a time, as it tends to **jump around from one thought to another like a monkey jumping around in its cage**. This is especially the case during times of stress when it defaults to negative thoughts that are then blown way out of proportion. When you are depressed you are not only thinking negative thoughts but you believe it. Your monkey is bound and determined to make you miserable and it knows exactly how to push your buttons. It is the monster of your mind and its sole purpose is your demise. **Because this is by far the most problematic aspect of our brain and the one that we absolutely cannot live with and be happy, it is the prime subject of this book.**

Yet another flaw of the brain is that it doesn't tell us when our body is dehydrated until it is almost too late and many have died as a consequence. Fortunately, we are now well aware of this problem and have educated ourselves to remember to drink fluids, especially in hot weather and or during strenuous activities, even though we may not feel thirsty in the least. Strangely enough, drinking too many fluids at one time can also result in death, which has also happened, albeit an extremely rare occurrence.

Additionally, our brain is way too easily tricked into believing that mind-altering substances such as alcohol, ecstasy, cocaine and heroin are absolutely necessary to feel "normal". Our brain associates a "positive feeling" with these substances; hence we are addicted. Unfortunately, as terrible as this problem is, this book does not even begin to address the solution to this problem. My only advice is to seek help as soon as possible from substance abuse professionals.

Okay, I am not a brain hater. Rather I just wanted to point out that it is far from perfect and it **needs a lot of help and understanding** which is one of the main purposes of this book.

Do you want to hear something good about our brain other than its protective reaction to physical pain? Well, our brain is unique in that it has an instinctive way of automatically adapting to new situations, i.e. background noise which may really annoy us initially will seem to lessen over time as our brain learns to essentially filter it out or ignore it completely. (My wife has often accused me of not listening to her, so I guess it really does work!)

As complex as the human body is with all of its parts and amazing functions, **it is actually our brain that totally dictates our entire life**, i.e.

what we do, how we do it, when we do it, where we do it and what we don't do. **Yes, our entire life's experience is a product of our brain.** Therefore, most of the focus of this book will be to **better understand its function and the consequences of the effectiveness of how it is functioning with the resulting affect on our happiness.**

It has been said that we only use 10% of our brain. Have you ever wondered what the other 90% is doing or what it was intended to do? If the 90% does exist, then is it possible for us to tap into just a small portion of it? If we could tap into just 10% of that 90% we would almost double the usable portion of our brain from 10 to 19%. Have you ever considered the impact of such a possibility? It could be quite remarkable. It might only take an additional 1% of the brain to expand our potential of more effectively operating our brain.

Albert Einstein and Edgar Cayce are both examples of those that have successfully tapped into a portion of their brain that was quite remarkable.

There were only a handful of scientists during Einstein's life that could even understand his theory of relativity, and even today his theory sounds crazy to most of us. His formula **(E=mc²)** looks like a very simple equation, but what it means is far from it. Essentially, mass can be produced from the void by shooting a beam of energy past an atomic nucleus, which then disappears and an electron and a positron appears in its place, i.e. **energy in the form of a beam has changed into the mass of two electrons**. He obviously tapped into a part of his brain that resulted in his genius, but to say that he was a genius is an understatement. It has been my understanding for years that the entire universe can be explained in complex mathematical terms, but who knew that mass times the speed of light squared is equal to energy? How does anyone possibly come up with this stuff anyway?

Even though Einstein was skeptical of religious beliefs as told in the Bible, he is quoted as having said, "Everyone who is seriously involved in the pursuit of science becomes convinced that a spirit is manifest in the laws of the universe, a Spirit vastly superior to that of man."

I also mentioned Edgar Cayce because his story is highly unusual but so well documented. He apparently had what could be called a telepathic or clairvoyant ability to read other people's minds. With literally volumes of well-documented cases of his medical diagnosis of other's medical condition and his prescription for their cure, it is almost impossible to summarily dismiss it as a hoax. Even Cayce couldn't explain it but he speculated that his brain could contact his subject's brain and it was actually the subject's brain that would communicate with his brain with medical information of what their body was lacking. If that wasn't strange enough, he went on to explain how his brain would then seek out the collective knowledge of the world's brains to find a cure for his ailing subjects. It was as if his brain was acting like a Google search engine. The results that he received while in a trance were often in Latin medical terms of which he had absolutely no understanding or knowledge. He said that it all started when he had apparently tapped into a different portion of his brain while he was deathly ill and in a coma. While still in a coma he told his doctors what his body needed in order to be cured. They followed his prescription and he was subsequently cured. From that point forward he realized his extraordinary brainpower and put it to use in helping others in poor health without asking for any compensation, so with no financial gain it is hard to believe that it was a scam.

Considering that most of us will never be able to tap into that 90% of our brain, we must rely on the 10% that we all possess to operate or control our conscious and subconscious thoughts, but the good news is that the 10% that we do have is more than enough to successfully obtain happiness **as long as we take the time to understand what is covered in this book and then put it into practice**. As smart as Einstein was it was commonly understood that he was far from happy so his extra brainpower did absolutely nothing to help him in his pursuit of happiness. It is my personal belief that he was so focused on exploiting his extra brainpower that he totally ignored the things that are being discussed in this book, which could have helped him in his pursuit of happiness.

CHAPTER 2
INSPIRATION

The Two Visitors:
Pain and Suffering

CHAPTER 2

INSPIRATION

I was greatly inspired to write this book by a poem and an essay written by my good friend, George Jaramillo. Both were written while in federal prison for two years with plenty of time to reflect on life; I affectionately liken this to his Tibetan Monk experience. (After serving his time he prevailed on appeal, which I discussed in great detail in my business book.) With his permission I am sharing his poem and essay.

His poem:

The Two Visitors

Pain visits uninvited, beyond control of man.
But, suffering comes upon us because we say it can.
The first one stays a short time or long we never know.
The second stays until we say it's time for you to go.
Pain makes a mess, yet in its wake there is value we can find.
But suffering only hurts us leaving nothing good behind.
So pain we should accept and move on with just a grin,
But suffering we should always try to never allow in.

George Jaramillo

Now for George's short essay explaining his poem in great detail:

In life pain is inevitable but suffering is not. Pain is axiomatic to our human condition. It arrives with us at birth, accompanies us at death and visits us sporadically all our days in between. Though all must experience pain, not all must suffer. The prevalence and intensity of our suffering is as individual and unique as the limitless causes of our pain.

Avoidance of pain is impossible but the avoidance of suffering is indispensable. The circumstances, which cause our pain, are distinct and vastly different from our perceptions of and reactions to them, which cause our suffering. While pain necessarily exists in our lives to teach us, suffering needlessly exists to punish us. It is a punishment of our own making and unlike pain it is completely within our control.

Pain offers life's most significant lessons and promotes the development of our highest human attributes. Strength only comes through the pain inducing agents of resistance and opposition; Wisdom is often gained through painful experience; Patience is developed by out-lasting difficulty or disappointment; Peace is found only after mental, emotional, spiritual or physical battles have been fought; And, faith is most fully developed when most fervently sought, usually during life's most painful moments. In stark contrast suffering is merely pain's by-product, literally a waste, offering us nothing useable or worthwhile.

Pain is definable and manageable. Suffering is the magnification of our pain. It is our pain as seen through the prism of our mind, which intensifies its vastness and camouflages its limits. Where pain is a real object, suffering is its projected image, seeming much larger, much more frightening and overwhelming than it really is.

Pain, however lengthy, is temporary, it begins and it ends. Suffering continues, as it is the prolongation of our pain. Like a child who needlessly suffers before and after the actual pain of an injection, many anticipate or cling to pain in a way that unnecessarily lengthens its tenure and deepens its impact in our lives.

So, it is our understanding of the difference between pain and suffering, our embracing of pain as necessary, the clarity with which we view it and the brevity with which we engage it, that will determine whether we are tempered by the refining lessons of our pain or we decompose in the worthless waste of our suffering.

George Jaramillo

CHAPTER 3

SUFFERING

We must be "mindful" of our suffering. Being mindful is awareness in the here and now.

CHAPTER 3

SUFFERING

"Suffering" is a word sometime used to describe physical pain; however, it more commonly refers to mental pain while the word "pain" usually refers to physical pain. Therefore, it is usually agreed that in life pain is inevitable, but suffering or mental pain is optional.

Physical pain is experienced through our conscious mind and involves emotional aspects while mental pain (suffering) is experienced most often through our subconscious minds; and, since it has subconscious emotions, it also involves physiological symptoms, like lethargy, headaches and nausea.

George is absolutely correct when he points out that pain offers us significant lessons. If you touch a hot stovetop your brain tells you to remove your hand as fast as possible to avoid further damage (an extremely valuable lesson that "pain" fortunately affords us). The pain from mental suffering does not have such an immediate or instantaneous reaction from our brain because this type of pain unfortunately goes unnoticed or is totally ignored unless we become **mindful or conscious of our suffering (awareness in the here and now)**. Just imagine how damaging and utterly stupid it would be if we ignored the pain and kept our hand on the stovetop. Once our mental pain or suffering is identified we must then take a proactive approach of **injecting positive thoughts** as nothing will happen automatically like it does with physical pain. The key to alleviating suffering is being **mindful or aware** that there is a problem that needs to be addressed.

According to the "Overlap Theory" based on Neuroimaging both physical pain and mental pain (suffering) share a common neurological basis in our brain despite being radically different types of pain. In other words, both physical and mental pain (suffering) actuates the same portion of our brain; so, from our brain's perspective they may be "almost" indistinguishable. My take on this is that they must be "somewhat" distinguishable because the brain responds immediately to physical pain but rarely if ever to the pain from suffering. (As you read further, you will see that both compassion for others and our personal pleasure also share a common place in our brain according to neuroscientists.)

Despite this pain overlap theory the medical field sharply and strongly distinguishes between pain and suffering and most of their attention goes just to the treatment of pain with millions upon millions of prescription drugs being issued every year fostering a drug addiction epidemic in this country. Maybe too much attention on "pain" while not nearly enough attention has been paid to what has become an epidemic of suffering with way too many suicides and murders being committed by mentally unbalanced or disturbed individuals, not to mention the ever increasing number becoming homeless and living on the streets. These are real-life social problems, which for the good of society must be more aggressively addressed. As you read a little further you will see how a heavy dose of compassion may be the only solution and why the practice of compassion can be the ultimate win/win solution due to how our brains are hard wired. Compassion begins with empathy and unfortunately the homeless as a whole are way too often viewed by society as being responsible for their own circumstances because of their poor decisions; therefore, there is not enough understanding and empathy to actually spur the required compassion from enough people to be able to effectively solve this problem. Unless and until society changes its view of the homeless, i.e. self inflicted substance abuse addicts, panhandlers, lifestyle choice by lazy people not willing to work etc., then it will always be an incredibly difficult uphill battle. Compassion for homeless stigmatized people with multiple and complex problems will always be infinitely more difficult to garner than for specific individuals; so, until "group think" changes, the homeless problem will need to be addressed one person at a time. Too bad there are not more compassionate people like my sister, Pat Hill, as she has been helping the homeless for years one individual at a time. She has a heart of gold, but I always worry about her safety. She is actually practicing compassion; and she will not have to enter Heaven before reaping her reward...yes, keep reading and you will clearly understand.

CHAPTER 4

FAITH

Having faith leads to peace of mind.

CHAPTER 4

FAITH

George speaks of Faith "being most fully developed when fervently sought, usually during life's most painful moments". I believe that potentially life-threatening situations give us all reason to pause and reflect on our own mortality. As a good friend once said, "None of us are getting out of here alive."

As a cancer survivor with a strong faith I can say that my immediate reaction to my diagnosis was absolutely one of peace. I prayed and I prayed often; however, I did not pray for life but rather prayed that God's Will results in my survival if and only if He had a higher and greater purpose for my life (possibly this book?). I was actually shocked at how quickly and easily I came to this conclusion. In fact, as I try to recall my thought process at that time, it was almost as if it was an instantaneous conclusion without any conscious thought process whatsoever; but, the one thing that I am 100% sure of is that I was totally at peace with whatever the outcome.

A fellow cancer patient, Teri, who has two children under the age of five, put it most succinctly when referring to her own stage 3 cancer when she said with a big smile which could light up a room, "It is what it is". Her calmness and total sense of peace really was quite remarkable and drew me to her in a way that I had never before experienced. She is dealing with her cancer in a very courageous, positive and pragmatic way which includes both chemotherapy and radiation therapy. As a nurse she helps others and as young mother her children need her, so I prayed for her then and continue to pray that God's Will results in her becoming a cancer survivor. If you are so inclined please offer up your prayers for her as well. Just pray for "Teri", God knows her by her first name.

The next best thing to being able to control things is to be able to accept things, because self-denial is self-destructive. Teri's matter of fact acceptance and positive attitude was very inspiring and was obviously a source of her calm courage and peace.

Having faith leads to peace and is only possible

by living in the here and now which then leads to the freedom to unload things that are outside of our control by placing them in God's hands as opposed to spending our lives worrying ourselves to death about them. **We will all die someday but how utterly ridiculous would it be to spend even a moment worrying about it?**

It has been my observation and personal experience that those who believe in God cope much better during stressful times. Essentially, instead of simply giving up on life, those with a strong belief in God will automatically place their fate in God's hands. This is much different than the negative thought process by which one gives up all hope; rather it releases their stress by placing their trust in God. An additional benefit of a belief in God is that believers have faith that there is a life after death. By placing their trust in God's hands does not necessarily mean a cure for one's ills but rather a result that is God's Will.

It has been said that, "Everyone wants to go to heaven, but no one wants to die to get there". Like everything in life, **if we can't control it**, then for our own mental health and happiness

we must accept it, and death clearly falls into that category.

Without a belief in God I believe that there can be no real peace of mind. One common belief in God is the existence of life after death, which can be very comforting as one contemplates his or her mortality.

Religion or the belief in God is based on faith - a conscious decision made using our brain. Early in one's life many don't use their brainpower to come to this conclusion; rather, they embrace their parents' belief or faith. I happen to have been born into a Catholic family and I am a practicing Catholic; however, I have often wondered if I had been born into a Jewish family would I be a practicing Jew today? Our brain obviously has the ability through education and research to change its belief (faith).

CHAPTER 5

THE EXISTENCE OF GOD

The importance of embracing God
in our life

CHAPTER 5

THE EXISTENCE OF GOD

Okay, proving the existence of God may seem like a tall order; but I remember a great story from grade school that has stayed with me for over 60 years. I found it to be extremely compelling and I hope to be able to do it justice. The story went something like this:

Visualize walking along the shoreline of a beach and coming across an elegant pocket watch that had washed up onto the shore. You pick it up and start to examine it carefully. You press on the stem and the back of the watch opens revealing all of its inner workings including a multitude of gears and springs in an impressive array that operates in a magical synchrony of movement. The face of the watch is equally as impressive with its crystal dial and exacting movement of the second, minute and hour hands. Next you notice that in addition to keeping the exact time of day it actually has a small window displaying the day of the month. You quickly realize how complex this watch really is and how talented the master watchmaker must obviously be.

Now you begin to question the existence of the master watchmaker and ponder the possibility that the watchmaker doesn't exist. You then rationalize the watch was actually created by the ocean with all of its materials from sand and seaweed to seashells and algae. Then, you simply add the motion of the waves that obviously was the agent or catalyst that brought all of the component parts together albeit over possibly millions of years and presto you have a watch, right? Yes, that's the ticket. Then you come to your senses and find it impossible to conclude anything other than the fact that a master watchmaker must have created the watch.

So now we can move on to our next mystery; namely, you now start to examine the human body with all of its component parts, from the brain, mouth, eyes, ears, nose, heart, lungs, kidney, liver, nervous system, veins, muscles, joints, ligaments, blood vessels, reproductive organs, hands, feet, legs and arms, to hundreds of other body aspects, like skin, a voice box, five senses, lymph nodes, DNA etc.

You then ponder the possibility that the human body could have been created by an accident of nature, like being washed up on an ocean beach with everything properly connected and in perfect working order. Once again you come to your senses and conclude just like with the watch that the human body, infinitely more complex than the watch, must also have had a maker or creator.

I have obviously been talking about the theory of random evolution as an alternative to God having created man. Over time the evolution of the human species has evolved in many different ways. From a physical standpoint we can clearly recognize our ancestral likeness, albeit somewhat better looking today, but that is subject to debate. What is absolutely unquestionable is the evolution of our brain, which is self-evident based on an incredible leap forward in our cognitive functions and technological abilities. How and why did our brain get smarter and why did it happen so quickly? Random evolution happens extremely slowly, but instead of a steady linear progression over long periods of time, our brains actually developed almost exponentially overnight in comparison. Was a more powerful brain necessary? If so it absolutely implies a reason or special intent for a future purpose, which implies some type of intelligence behind the intent, like a creator. Highly accelerated evolution without an intelligent being behind it strains credulity, as the evolution of our brain was anything but random. Why did other species not evolve anywhere near as fast as humans? Not even close. Other than the question about our brain, the biggest question I have is how did we develop the ability to speak through a random evolutionary process? Was an ability to speak necessary for a special intent for a future purpose? If so, this too implies some type of intelligence behind the intent as well. If God wanted us to have a more capable brain, then how ineffective would it be if none of us could talk? Without verbal communication it is hard to believe that we would have been able to use our newfound brainpower to accomplish all that we have accomplished, including but not limited to putting a man on the moon for example.

If God wanted to take credit for our existence He could have simply had all of the religions of the world chronicle our creation as having evolved from the apes, which He could say He created.

But He didn't. Instead, all of the religions have chronicled an unmistakable clear-cut message that God created us "first hand" from the get-go. Please keep in mind that a belief in evolution does not disprove the existence of God but I find it absolutely impossible to embrace, as a belief in the random evolution of man would require a tremendous amount of faith. In fact, as far as faith goes, I believe that it takes infinitely more faith to believe that there is no God than to believe that there is a God.

Additionally, I don't see a downside in believing in a loving God. The **benefits are many** including having an outline of what is acceptable and what is not via the Ten Commandments and other teachings in the Bible, not to mention the hope for not just a life after death but for the greatest life possible. Please note that I included the Ten Commandments as an actual "benefit" with all of its "Thou Shalt Nots". I am sure many would love to be able to pick and choose just 7 or 8 out of the 10 to obey; however, it has been my observation that life is much easier with rules that make you a better person. I don't believe in a Hell; but, if there actually is one, it may very well be here on earth based on the personal consequences of our bad decisions, like incarceration, fines, depression, guilt, anxiety, regret etc. Obeying rules makes for a better life that is free of guilt and other negative consequences.

Speaking of Hell, the Catholic faith no longer preaches "Hell fire and damnation" as it had many years ago when I was growing up. I believe this to be a very good thing because it is a negative motivator and only a strong positive motivator should be the basis for the exercise of our free will in deciding right from wrong and the resulting love for our neighbor and for a loving God.

"We must believe in free will. We have no choice." Isaac B. Singer

Essentially, evil is necessary because without it we would not have free will (impossible), and without free will there could not be an opportunity for growth leaving no chance to become all that God wanted us to be.

On the topic of Hell, several years ago a priest told a story of the days when the Church did practice "Hell fire and damnation", and the story went like this:

*A priest addressed his congregation on a Sunday morning and started off by saying, "Everyone in this parish will be going to Hell unless you change your ways." Having said that he noticed that a gentleman in the third pew was giggling, so he decided to repeat his message, but a little louder this time as he said, **"Absolutely every single member of this parish will be going to Hell unless you change your ways."** With that he could not help but notice that the gentleman was laughing uncontrollably; so being very indignant the priest very loudly addressed him directly and said, **"Why do you find this so funny?"** and he responded, "I am not from this parish."*

CHAPTER 6

CONQUERING SELF

The power of the mind is the power
of positive thinking.

CHAPTER 6

CONQUERING SELF

"The first and best victory is to conquer self. To be conquered by self is, of all things, the most shameful and vile." Plato

So it begs the question; namely, how do we conquer self and what does that mean anyway?

Well, Plato is actually talking about conquering or controlling our brain. **Successful people conquer their brain by being positive thinkers**. Unless we take a proactive approach to our thought process, then our brain will automatically default to negative or self-destructive thoughts. It is sad that this is the default position of our brain, but knowing this will allow us to take corrective action before these negative thoughts are blown way out of proportion leading to mental suffering in the form of anxiety or depression. We must be

continuously mindful of what is happening with our monkey so that conscious efforts of positive thoughts can be exerted to overcome and control or tame it. It wants you to feel depressed and anxious. It will distort how bad past experiences have been and how frightening future experiences will be...certainly not your friend, so you can't afford to ignore it; to do so will be at your own peril; however, this won't be easy as it is great at hiding outside your conscious mind. It can only be defeated by **being aware of its activities and thinking positive thoughts**; left to its own devises it will make you absolutely miserable, guaranteed.

Since you have been living with your monkey all of your life, you have become so accustomed to its presence that it is a "normal" part of your every day life. It is so well concealed that it has become part of who you have become; albeit the worst part manifesting itself in anger, hatred, anxiety, fear, sadness or depression and jealousy. A typical negative response of our monkey is to blame something external to us for our self-destructive attitude, i.e. "I was so mad that 'it' drove me to drink." Of course "it" is actually, you guessed it, your ever-present monkey. You may feel justified in blaming others, but ultimately it is always your fault, as **others cannot control your thoughts, only you can.**

"I didn't say it was your fault, I said I was blaming you." Anonymous

Once again, the first step is to be **aware or mindful** of what your monkey is up to. It then becomes **your choice** to either take corrective action or not. As an example, if you are upset with someone, your monkey will demand that you focus on that person's shortcomings ad nausea sacrificing your mental health. None of us are perfect, so ignore your monkey and **consciously** start focusing on that person's best qualities (even the worst of us have some good qualities). Your mental health comes first, so block out the negative and focus on the positive.

If you want to experience living in the moment (the here and now), try eating a hot fudge sundae or any other guilty pleasure while enjoying every single spoonful. This is commonly referred to as "comfort food" and those who struggle with emotional problems of depression and anxiety find solace in eating comfort food because it is a way to live in the present and find temporary joy and happiness. This "solution" has led to another epidemic of obesity; so, an attempt to cure an emotional problem actually backfires big time because it just creates a problem with our physical health. This in turn adds to our mental health problems in the form of disappointment, depression and frustration, which our monkey will gladly exploit to the max.

Plato really knew what he was talking about, since without what he calls this **"first and best victory"** in conquering self, we would become dysfunctional as nothing else in life would matter because all would be lost in our **continuous state of anxiety and or depression**.

The saddest thing of all...all of your suffering is 100% self-inflicted. As George stated in his essay, "suffering is a punishment of our own making and unlike pain it is completely within our control." Your internal self-abuse comes from illogical distorted thinking. Your brain will tell you that "what happened" was terrible and that you are well justified in being upset, disappointed or disgusted over this terrible thing; **but, get over it and move on with your**

life. As each day passes all of those disasters are further and further in the past and there is absolutely no upside to living in the past.

There is a lot of truth in the following quote from Lao Tzu (A great Chinese philosopher):

If you are depressed, you are living in the past. If you are anxious, you are living in the future. If you are at peace, you are living in the present.

If you are depressed then you are allowing your brain (thoughts) to live in the past. Essentially you are hashing and rehashing problems or mistakes of the past ad nauseam fomenting feelings of guilt, regret and depression. Depression will keep you from thinking clearly which prevents you from putting things in proper perspective.

If you are anxious then you are allowing your brain to live in the future constantly worrying about events that may or may not occur.

If you are at peace, then you are allowing your brain to live in the present. We can't change the past and we certainly can't predict the future.

We can, however, learn from the past and plan for the future; but we cannot allow our brain to be obsessed with either.

Like most things, this advice is a lot easier said than done as our brain can take on a life of its own without cognitive approval from us. Our brain is like a monkey jumping around from one thought to another despite our effort to concentrate on just one thing.

The power of the mind, or more commonly referred to as "mind over matter" is a real thing. Don't think so? Then how does one explain the placebo effect, which approximates 25% of those who benefited from a placebo? **The power of the mind is the power of positive thinking.**

Okay, so all we need to do is to simply think positive thoughts, right? Yes, but with so many other things in life, "It is easier said than done." If it were easy we would not have so many committing suicide. We would not have so many alcoholics and drug addicts. They are all victims of negative thoughts invariably leading to bad decisions and mental suffering.

Mental health of varying degrees is an epidemic in this country and not enough is being done to address this problem. Hence my motivation to write this book designed to reach those who wish to be proactive with their own mental health through a self-help process. To be perfectly clear, I am not talking about those who have a mental illness requiring professional help, rather about all the rest of us who could use a little help or advice in coping with the ubiquitous human condition of our brain.

The human brain unfortunately does not come with an owner's manual, a warranty or even a maintenance schedule. So how do we successfully operate such a complex and highly sophisticated computer? How do we deal with change, fear, disappointment, health issues and the knowledge of our own mortality?

CHAPTER 7
MEDITATION

Finding calmness and sanity

CHAPTER 7

MEDITATION

There is a lot to be said about the positive effects of meditation. Steve Jobs attributed it to his creative and revolutionary ideas in the field of computers and the ability to communicate with each other around the world considered impossible or even crazy just 30 years ago. Our i-Phones today have one thousand more times the computing ability of the IBM 360 super computer that put us on the moon 50 years ago. Those computers filled up an entire room and now we have computers a thousand times more powerful that we can carry around in our pants' pocket.

Meditation can also be a great method for relaxing our brain and if done correctly it can free our mind of our ever-present monkey's activities. This is a great place to find calmness and sanity.

CHAPTER 8
THE POWER OF POSITIVE THINKING

"Happiness is just a state of mind"

CHAPTER 8

THE POWER OF POSITIVE THINKING

Successful people control their brain by being positive thinkers; but, for most of us, it is not so easy, primarily because it is human nature to blow things way out of proportion exacerbating one's ability to think positive thoughts. It is difficult if not impossible to control negative thoughts while in the throws of bad news. The loss of a job is certainly not an inconsequential event and can have a paralyzing affect on us. How can anything good come from this?

I highly recommend reading "The Power of Positive Thinking" by Norman Vincent Peal. The glass is always at least half full. You can either decide to be positive and focus on the upside or you can be negative and focus on the downside. And guess what, **the choice is 100% yours**. Just like most things in life, **you can either be happy, or not, depending on**

your perspective. Keep in mind that success and happiness can be mutually exclusive, as **our happiness does not depend on our success and our success does not necessarily bring us happiness.**

Your success should be measured in terms of your happiness and not by your financial wealth. Keep in mind that you will find happiness not only in possessing but also in doing. If your success or wealth does not translate to happiness, then it is absolutely worthless; however, happiness can nonetheless be found in the process of accumulating wealth with all of its exciting challenges.

It is great to have long-term goals, but **we all live in the present, so that is where we must find our happiness.** In other words, take one step at a time and enjoy **every single day** of the journey. As a great philosopher once said, "It is not the destination, but the journey that is most important." Our happiness must be found in the satisfaction we find in our daily lives with its own immediate rewards. **Never postpone your happiness and never tell yourself that you will be happy when, because "when" is in the future and none of us live there. Living**

in the future is inviting unwanted anxiety into your life. Furthermore, your monkey is essentially telling you that you can't be happy with your current circumstances. How sad of a lie is that? Another problem is that even if the future happiness-generating event happens, it will only be a temporary celebration as is the case with virtually everything in life. You will then establish your next "when" in a never-ending pursuit of an ever-elusive happiness. We must make our happiness a **daily occurrence** no way reliant on any external event that may or may not happen.

Dale Carnegie put it best when he said, **"Success is getting what you want. Happiness is wanting what you get." Don't think about what you don't have, but rather focus on what you do have and embrace it.** And don't make other people responsible for your happiness because then it is in their hands and not yours, where it should be. Don't be irresponsible with the responsibility for your happiness. After all, **"happiness is just a state of mind"**. Yes, it actually is as simple as that, as **you and you alone can create and control your thoughts or state of mind.**

As an example, let's say you are driving to work and get a flat tire, which will make you late for work. Well, you can choose to either let this experience completely ruin your day by being in a rotten mood, or you can be happy because the flat tire did not cause an accident, or because your spare was not flat, or because it didn't happen on the freeway, or because it wasn't raining, or simply because you had been lucky not to have had a flat tire in more than 7 years (flats happen).

Every situation in life is relative: things could always be worse so there really are a lot of things to be thankful for but we must actively think about them and not simply take them for granted, as most people will do. **The perfect and ageless example is the guy who was upset because he had no shoes until he saw a man who had no feet**.

Albert Einstein once said, **"The true value of a human being is determined primarily by the measure and the sense in which he has attained liberation from the self."**

What is he talking about when he says, "liberation from the self"? Well, I believe that he is talking about liberating our self from our mental addictions. If you always make your desires a preference and not an addiction you will not be setting yourself up for agonizing frustration and disappointment. **Addictions make you a slave. Making your desires preferences may be the single most important aspect of living a happy life.** You must be willing to let go of something that you desire before you can be at peace. We cannot and must not stay in the selfish world of self.

Albert Einstein also said, **"There are only two ways to live your life. One is as though nothing is a miracle. The other is as if everything is."**

Miracles are obviously of a spiritual nature; and, if we are all spiritual beings there must be a little bit of God in all of us, right? I had always been taught in my religion that God gives us unconditional love and He wants us to love one another as we love ourselves. This concept of love is not too difficult to practice with select family members or friends but how does it work with total strangers? Do we actually have the capacity for empathy, or love and compassion for others that is genuine? If so, then it must come from our spiritual being. Thinking outside the conscious brain takes us to the spiritual world begging the question, how does one get there? I believe there is only one way and that is through our **practice of love and compassion for each other**, the two basic tenants of the Gospels and the teachings of Jesus. If you try it you will like it, **guaranteed**. No, I don't guarantee it, but your brain does because that is how we are all hard wired. You just need to keep reading to see why.

CHAPTER 9

COMPASSION

"Compassion is a necessity,
not a luxury"

CHAPTER 9

COMPASSION

Compassion is the response in our brain to the suffering of others that actually motivates us to desire to help them. Compassion is more than simple empathy as compassion gives rise to an active desire to alleviate another's suffering **which then requires actual action**; hence, compassion is almost universally considered as among the greatest virtues by all major religions and philosophies.

In the Sermon on the Mount, Jesus gave us assurance that, **"Blessed are the merciful, for they shall obtain mercy."** This can be restated as, "Blessed are the compassionate, for they shall obtain compassion". Additionally, in the Parable of the Good Samaritan He stresses the virtue of being compassionate, and the Gospels even extend true compassion to one's enemies.

The Dalai Lama once said that, **"Compassion is a necessity, not a luxury".** He also said that, **"It is a question of human survival".** Basically, he is saying our compassion helps us connect with others, which can lead to increased motivation or an increase in our desire in trying to do something in an effort to relieve the pain and suffering of others.

To be perfectly clear, if you wish to practice compassion for others, it is not good enough to feel sorry for them, or to have pity on them or empathy for them; but rather, you must take a **proactive approach** whereby you **actually take steps** to reduce or eliminate someone's pain or suffering whether it be physical pain or mental suffering.

CHAPTER 10

NEUROPSYCHOLOGY AND COMPASSION

We are innately wired to help the suffering of others.

CHAPTER 10

NEUROPSYCHOLOGY AND COMPASSION

Neuroscientists, Jill Rilling and Gregory Berns at Emory University, have found that performing compassionate acts actually activates the same area of our brain associated with pleasure and reward. They therefore concluded that **people are innately wired to want to help alleviate the suffering of others via the practice of compassion and the positive feeling one then experiences in helping others.**

As I am writing this it dawned on me that I have actually experienced a great amount of pleasure and reward in my management positions by practicing compassion through leadership in the workplace. As an example, I offer a story from my previous business book. Little did I know at the time that I wrote these words that I would be revisiting this story as an example of how the practice of compassion actually resulted in my receiving pleasure or a **great sense of comfort**.

The title of this story is 'Know What Your Employees Want':

What is an employee's highest priority? How would you rank their priorities? I have found that how you rank your employee's priorities is the key to successfully manage and keep good employees. Would you say that an employee's top priority is pay? If you said yes, then you would be wrong. Would you say it is the people that they work with? Once again, you would be wrong. How about the type of work? Well, you are getting warmer, but still wrong. Don't even say vacation time or other benefits as they are not even in the top four.

An employee's top priority is job security. Yes, everyone would like more money, but nobody wants to worry about not having a job. I know that this may seem obvious but it is surprising to me how few managers actually capitalize on this knowledge of their employee's basic and top priority. Moreover, there are two additional priorities ahead of pay level for most employees: the type of work they perform and the people with whom they work.

Job security is an employee's top priority; however, depending on the economy and more specifically how it affects his or her place of employment, job security may or may not be their top concern.

It is usually only during tough economic times that an employee's top priority of job security becomes his or her top concern. In other words, employees are not always preoccupied with losing their job, but job security is nonetheless their top priority. Only those who are either overconfident or foolhardy will throw caution to the wind at their own peril. This is the reason why most employees will either not ask for a raise or will not be too aggressive in asking for one.

So, how do you give your employees job security? Well, favorable comments and giving deserved credit are a great start. In fact, this has often been considered more valuable to an employee than a raise because favorable feedback reinforces one's self-esteem and value to the company, which creates a great sense of job security. It should go without saying that an employee who does not have a sense of job security will be looking for a new job. An employee's job security will also help reduce employee turnover. Complimenting job performance also improves employee morale and better job performance. I have been amazed at how few managers praise their employees.

Once I asked a manager why he would always criticize his employees when needed but never praised them. His shocking response was that he was afraid to praise them for fear of having them ask for a raise and it was his job to keep the cost down!

During a severe economic downturn, I needed to reduce production by 20%. I could have simply informed our employees via a memo that business was lousy and we needed to layoff 20% of our employees. Unfortunately, with a 10% unemployment rate at the time, I knew that any laid off employees would have a difficult time finding other employment. Consequently, I gathered all 500 employees and very passionately explained that I didn't want to lose a single employee, as we valued each and every one of them. I told them that I would rather have some employees leave for other employment opportunities than to have to lay off someone who may not be able to find other employment. Therefore, in lieu of a 20% layoff, I announced that we would be cutting back their hours by 20% via a 4-day workweek. I was absolutely shocked by their standing ovation. Okay, to be honest, even though they were standing and applauding, we only had 10 chairs in the plant so everyone was already standing. Nonetheless, it was a great moment and technically speaking it actually was a "standing ovation"!

*I made no promises of how long the reduced hours would last, but I told them if enough employees voluntarily left for other jobs, this attrition would benefit the remaining employees by offering them increased hours. We ended up losing only a few employees and a number of employees were able to find part-time jobs on Fridays or Saturdays to make up for their reduced pay. This approach not only increased morale due to eliminating an anticipated layoff during very uncertain times, but it also brought us closer together. I also made it clear that all of the office staff and management were on a reduced pay program and that no one was going to have their pay reinstated unless everyone was reinstated, as we were all in this together for better or for worse. Having had to layoff a number of employees during my career, I found that this approach gave me **a great sense of***

comfort. *Keep in mind that firing someone for cause is always difficult; however, it is infinitely more difficult to layoff good employees through no fault of their own.*

*During that meeting I shared the company's business plan and status, which subsequently lead to our employees asking me to give them monthly updates and I agreed. These updates were a great stepping-stone for not only **helping alleviate their anxiety** but also to form an even closer bond; one built on trust and honesty.*

*Loyalty is a two-way street. You cannot expect employees to be loyal to the company if it is not loyal to them in return. **Treating your employees, as you would like to be treated is a great policy.***

In retrospect, I now realize that I was actually practicing a principle of compassion manifested in the social context as altruism. I was actually applying the so-called Golden Rule with its implication of compassion with the expression: **"Do unto others as you would have them do unto you."**

No wonder I was such a happy camper during my entire career as every time I did something for the benefit of my employees, I actually benefitted personally.

But who knew?

The Dalai Lama put it best when he said, **"If you want others to be happy, practice compassion.   If you want to be happy, practice compassion."** Wow, can you connect the dots and see the exact correlation to what the neuroscientists are telling us about the brain? Yes, the same part of the brain stimulated by being compassionate is the same part that gives us pleasure and reward, truly a win/win outcome.

Based on this conclusion, I surmise that Mother Teresa must have been the happiest or one of the happiest people that has ever lived, despite my understanding that she may have suffered from depression.   However, her happiness did not come easy, as it required hard work, unimaginable hard work. It begs the question; namely, how happy do you want to be, and what effort are you willing to invest in order to maximize your own happiness? This is a very straightforward question and the solution is neither technical nor beyond our ability to clearly comprehend. All it takes is a commitment and a plan of action. Wow, this compassion for others might be a great way to become happy without actually working on controlling our monkey, right? No, not if you wish to be happy all of the time. The only time that you can experience peace and happiness is in the present, or in the here and now. **Remember that depression and regret are found in the past and anxiety and uncertainty are found in the future.** The only place that any of us can live is in the present. Living otherwise will gain you nothing but misery; there is no upside whatsoever. **Living in the present and being happy all of the time will always require conscious thought in the monitoring of your monkey's activities. This is true despite how happy we are occasionally from time to time by practicing compassion.**

CHAPTER 11

HATE

"Resentment is like drinking poison and hoping it will kill your enemies."

CHAPTER 11

HATE

I wanted to briefly mention hate because it is such a strong emotion and because it is the opposite of love and compassion. Put very simply, love and compassion make us feel great whereas hate destroys us. Nelson Mandela put it best when he said, **"Resentment (or hatred) is like drinking poison and hoping it will kill your enemies."**

You and only you can control your feelings and only positive thoughts can overcome a feeling of hatred. Understanding this and taking proactive action to get over this strong emotion may prove to be one of the best things that you can do for your own mental wellbeing. As the Beatles said, "Let it be, let it be". Wow, finding a lot of wisdom all over the place!

CHAPTER 12

HANDLING STRESS

"God, grant me the serenity to accept the things that I cannot change, the courage to change the things that I can, and the wisdom to know the difference"

CHAPTER 12

HANDLING STRESS

I believe that a certain amount of stress can actually be a good thing. We will all experience stressful events of great magnitude in our life so how do we prepare ourselves to handle it? If you have never encountered any stress prior to a tremendously stressful event it can be absolutely debilitating. I believe that like most things in life we need to know how to handle smaller doses of stress during our lifetime in order to help us cope with major stressful events when they happen. What we need to do is sort things out as we go and try to gain valuable insight from those who have preceded us. In "How to Stop Worrying and Start Living," Dale Carnegie stated a great truth: **"When something bad happens it is human nature for our brain to blow the situation way out of proportion. Things are usually never as bad as first imagined."** Carnegie's advice was to rationally visualize how bad a situation could possibly be and then be able to **accept it**. The worst-case will probably never happen; however, if you prepare for it and know that you can survive it, you will then realize a tremendous amount of comfort knowing that you can handle the worst-case scenario. Your objective is to improve your situation by whatever means possible. This will never be a simple process; but at least your brain will be in a calmer state of mind, which is always best for effective problem solving.

"If you think things can't get any worse it's probably only because you lack sufficient imagination." Anonymous

As an example of how I handled my first major stressful event, I offer the following:

I had been the president of a company that was successfully and voluntarily liquidated in 1991; however, a year after moving on to my next job I was served personally with a $500,000 lawsuit in a Chicago, Illinois Federal Court under RICO (Racketeer Influenced and Corrupt Organizations Act), which is a law specifically designed to bring organized Mafia crime bosses to justice. It certainly was enough to ruin my day, to say the very least. Not being any different than most people faced with this lawsuit, I was absolutely devastated. As a newly hired vice president and chief financial officer of a failing public company, I was so involved in my new job that I couldn't fathom how I could possibly have the time to prove my innocence, and by law, I only had 30 days to answer the complaint or lawsuit that was filed against me. My emotions or thoughts racing through my mind included being upset, mad and very concerned. All three of these thoughts were separate and distinct emotions that needed to be rationally confronted. Being upset was based on the shock of having to spend time and money proving my innocence. Being mad was based on the fact that all of the allegations were totally false. Being very concerned was based on the possibility that I might be found guilty. So, I saw that I had two choices; namely, roll over and die, or fight for my life. Not unlike most people my mind was blowing things way out of proportion despite the fact that I was absolutely innocent. My mind kept defaulting to the negative possibility that innocent people are sometime found guilty with the resulting consequences of losing my house and even the possibility of filing for bankruptcy; not comforting thoughts. Feeling anxious and depressed my thoughts were dominated by a pervasive negativity, but what was even worse was I started to believe things could really be as bad as I was imaging, so I needed to start doing something proactively, just like I had done many times in running a troubled business.

First I decided on fighting for my life and quickly therefore now prepared to calm down and reread the twenty-page complaint without being emotionally upset with the same clarity that I had while handling dozens of lawsuits filed against companies I had previously worked for over the prior twenty years. This worked well; but having reread it I was still both mad and very concerned. Furthermore, after rereading it one more time while writing notes in the margins, I was still mad. Finally, I decided that focusing on being outraged was not a solution to my problem; so, I focused 100% of my emotions on the positive action of proving my innocence. My mindset was so focused in solving this problem that I had no time to be mad; however, I was still very concerned to the point of not being able to rest until I knew that I would be able to prove my innocence. My monkey was way out of control. Consequently,

I spent six to seven hours every night after work until about one or two in the morning answering all of the complaints lodged against me. Since the allegations were made regarding verbal communications made several years earlier, it was incumbent on me to recollect all of my conversations with the plaintiff, not an easy task. Fortunately, even though I have a very good memory, I still actually surprised myself in being able to recall every single detail of our past conversations. After three nights of pouring over the plaintiff's allegations I had answered every single complaint and was extremely pleased with my comprehensive answers. It was only after I had done all that I could to prove my innocence that I was able to completely relax and turn to the next task of finding an attorney in Chicago. If I was not able to overcome my fear, or tame my monkey, then I would not have been able to rationally help myself reduce the downside risk.

To dispel any thought that I am a crook, I felt compelled to provide you with the outcome of this lawsuit as follows:

After a year I was totally exonerated on all counts and the judge was so outraged by the false allegations made against me that he sanctioned the plaintiff's attorney and threw out the case. Not only was I reimbursed for my legal fees from the plaintiff's attorney, the judge ordered the court records to reflect that all of the allegations made against me were found to be totally false. He said that he did this to keep the false allegations from reflecting badly on my character in the event that I ever decided to run for public office (fat chance). Keep in mind that all court records are subject to public scrutiny.

In the above example the source of my stress was self-evident; however, I offer a second example whereby I was not even mindful of what my monkey was up to. All that I knew at the time was that I became nauseated every Sunday evening; I was clueless as to why since I had always been highly proficient at problem solving and didn't think that it was due to mental stress. I finally rationalized it must have been something I had eaten, right? Wrong! My monkey had actually been working overtime without my cognitive permission and I was suffering.

Well, like most executives I have always been motivated by a fear of failure. Basically, business is never a static situation and therefore all executives will encounter both good and bad times in their career. What defines the success or failure of an executive is how he or she handles the tough times. For the successful executive, it is fear of failure that is the greatest motivator; if you are not afraid to fail, you are not committed to succeed. My fear of failure was so compelling that it consumed me in both time and thought. Because I loved the challenge of solving problems and even find it exhilarating, I never thought it could possibly cause me stress. Well, every Sunday evening at 6 pm, like clockwork, I would start getting a nauseating headache; but, I never understood why until years later when I reflected upon some very stressful times over the course of my career. What I came to realize was that during the week I never had a headache, I was way too busy solving problems, which kept my body and mind busy actively interacting with people and solving problems. The adrenalin rush or endorphins that were released from this challenging activity was absolutely exhilarating and precluded any possibility of having a headache. I then realized that my problem on Sunday nights was that I started thinking about my next day's activities. **Yes, I was living in the future** with all of its anxiety and uncertainty. The anticipation of what I was going to do and the possible outcomes consumed me. Furthermore, there was no rush of adrenalin or endorphins being released because I was not able to put anything into action until the next day. It was the frustration over the inactivity that resulted in my stress related nauseating headaches. I was not being mindful of what my monkey was up to, that is, steering me down a path headlong into needless mental pain (suffering). In retrospect, I should have occupied my time in the gym to release endorphins, which I subsequently ended up doing later in my career. Exercising and being physically tired not only helped shut down my brain but it also guaranteed me a good night's sleep. Fortunately, I eventually learned this (I was just disappointed that it took me so long). Henceforth, I became extremely **mindful** of the critical importance of knowing what my monkey was up to and keeping it on a short leash; otherwise, my health would be in dire jeopardy in a stressful career of turning around troubled companies.

It is critical to deal with problems in a positive way regardless of how effective the outcome. There will always be problems in your life and they need to be addressed, but **the absence of problems doesn't make one happy**. You will not be able to control everything in your life. The next best thing however is to be willing to **accept things**. This philosophy can be summed up in the following Serenity Prayer:

God, grant me the serenity to accept the things that I cannot change, the courage to change the things that I can, and the wisdom to know the difference.

Serenity is simply a sense of peace only to be found by living in the present.

We must accept what we cannot change. So what can we change? We certainly can change ourselves; however, we need the courage to change, which is never easy. As an example, if you are an alcoholic or a drug addict, then it will take a tremendous amount of courage and effort in order to kick your habit. It would be a waste of time and effort to attempt to change things that are beyond our control, but changing ourselves is well within our control. What we need is to **develop love and compassion for ourselves,** which we all know requires us to make a commitment and to take positive actions to alleviate our suffering **just as we would do in showing compassion for others**.

What else can we change? We can help change others if they have the courage and the will. Unfortunately, sometimes in life there are people with substance abuse addictions whom we cannot help since they are either incapable or unwilling to help themselves.

CHAPTER 13

GIVING YOUR BRAIN

VERBAL COMMANDS

You must command your brain
to respond to less than desirable
results in a positive manner.

CHAPTER 13

GIVING YOUR BRAIN VERBAL COMMANDS

To keep your brain from automatically defaulting to negative thoughts, which can quickly lead to a state of depression or anxiety, **you must command your brain to respond to less than desirable results in a positive manner**. I have found that by verbalizing the command it has a better chance of sinking in. I have also found that it is critical to repeat the command on a regular basis, as your brain tends to have a short memory if you don't.

Here is a great example taken from my book "How To Succeed In Business By Really Trying" it having garnered extremely favorable comments on how to avoid depression associated with failure and guilt as it relates to being a procrastinator:

Having the discipline to develop and maintain good work habits will obviously serve you well but how do we do that? Well, the more difficult the task the greater the chances are that we will be a procrastinator even though we are generally not. Obviously, we do the things we like and don't do the things that we don't like. As an example, we all know that exercise can be very beneficial to our health but most of us hate to work out; so, very few will actually force themselves to develop the habit of working-out on a regular basis. We all know that New Year's resolutions usually don't last very long despite our best intentions. So why is that? Well, your success is inversely proportional to the level of its difficulty. In other words, the easier the task the greater your success rate, but the more difficult the task the less successful you will be. Since most "resolutions" are objectives that we have already tried before and failed, we are predisposed to fail again because our mind-set is that it is simply too difficult. If a task were made less difficult, our chances of success would be greater, right? Okay, this is obvious enough but how does this knowledge help? I wanted to get into the habit of working-out in the gym for an hour every other day. Even though the workouts were exhilarating, after a few weeks I found more than enough excuses to not workout for the rest of my life! My best excuse was that I was just too damn tired, period. Okay, maybe I will try it again next January. Yes, that ugly word "try" which we all know is not a real commitment.

A financial incentive should be an effective means of attaining our goal, at least that's what my good friends, Ken and Karen, thought. They told me that if they simply paid for a two-year gym membership that they would be obligated to go; but, after just one workout, they simply couldn't find the time. About a year later the urge to exercise returned, especially since they had already spent the money; so, they got their workout gear together and drove to the gym. Unfortunately, they couldn't find the gym. After circling the block several times they realized that the building had been torn down and the gym was out of business! At least they didn't feel guilty for not working out!

Okay, now for the solution. I found that the secret to success was to reduce the difficulty level of your objectives to make them less daunting. I realized that just thinking about getting ready and going to the gym to work out for an hour was mentally exhausting. And the more that I failed to workout, the worse I felt; a little guilty and a lot more depressed which made me even more tired and just reinforced my reason for not working out in the first place. I just saw it as a bad idea, period. How is that for a great excuse? And believe me, I had plenty more. In any event, the solution was actually a mental trick so that I would not feel badly about not working out. I simply reduced the difficulty level of my objective; I promised myself that I would workout just 5 minutes every other day and only more if I felt like it, so a longer workout was totally optional. This is what I call a no guilt, no failure commitment. How big of a loser would I be if I couldn't keep this easy commitment? Well, there are two things that I already knew: one, I always felt great both physically and mentally after an hour workout; two, and more importantly, I knew that once I started working-out, regardless of how tired I felt beforehand, both the blood flow and the endorphins would kick in and I would want to continue to workout for an entire hour. I ended up working out for an entire hour at least 9 out of 10 times, even if I had a slight headache or felt dead tired beforehand. And the times that I only worked out for just 5 minutes I didn't feel guilty or depressed. This no guilt, no failure workout has been working great for me for 16 years now and counting.

*As a cautionary note, **I have found it necessary to continually remind myself every day before going to the gym that it will be just a 5 minute workout as it will always be an ongoing process because it is simply way too easy to fail, especially as one gets older.***

Remember to just get started and don't overwhelm yourself with the magnitude of the entire task.

"A journey of a thousand miles starts with a single step." Lao-Tzu

CHAPTER 14
TESTING YOUR HAPPINESS

It is importance to monitor your inner monkey on a continuous basis.

CHAPTER 14

TESTING YOUR HAPPINESS

As a quick overview, my self-help advice incorporates the following **five indispensable elements** for your pursuit of happiness:

1) First, an understanding and recognition of our flawed brain with its negative default settings and the need to be **mindful** or aware of what our inner monkey is up to and how destructive it can be in our lives.

2) The need for a proactive approach to our mental health via **positive thinking**.

3) The importance of **embracing God** in our lives with His unconditional love.

4) The importance of **living in the present**, which is the only place to find peace and happiness.

5) The importance of practicing **love and compassion** in an attempt to relieve the pain and suffering of others.

If you embrace these five elements by putting them in practice right now, then your happiness will begin right now (no waiting required). "Right now" is the "present" and the only place that we all live, so why wait to be happy? Don't worry about being happy tomorrow because that is not the here and now and we can't live there until tomorrow and tomorrow may never come.

As a test of your current state of happiness, if you are not feeling good about life, smiling or laughing **every single moment of today**, then you need to work harder on your **pursuit** of happiness. The word "pursuit" means that you must exert some effort, which is the opposite of doing nothing or being lazy. If you are depressed or feeling badly, then I know that it will be difficult to start thinking positive thoughts, but you must get started now for your own good. You will be the sole beneficiary of all of your efforts, so just do it for yourself because you deserve it.

In speaking of being happy I said, "every single moment of today" for two reasons; namely, today means the **present** and every single moment means **right now** as you are reading this. If it is not moment-to-moment you will not be **mindful** of what your inner monkey is doing **every single second of the day**, which is always counterproductive to your happiness. So the bottom line is that you **must be mindful or monitor your inner monkey on a continuous basis** and not just every once in a while. As a self-test, **become mindful right now** by asking yourself if you are happy. If your answer is no, ask yourself if you are depressed about the past or anxious about the future? If your answer is yes to either, you will need to **start living in the present** and **start thinking positive thoughts** immediately and continue doing so on an ongoing basis while **constantly monitoring your monkey**. Also, if you have not already done so, **embrace God in your life** and start practicing **compassion** by helping others with their pain and suffering. To help reinforce your commitment to your happiness, I would suggest that you reread sections of this book on an ongoing basis.

Thank You for reading my book as it is my sincere hope that it will actually have a favorable impact on your mental outlook and ultimately your pursuit of happiness.

EPILOGUE
Inspiration and Passion

EPILOGUE

In writing this book, which I had been thinking about doing for a long time, I prayed for inspiration, as I was experiencing "writer's block". In other words, after I wrote down the title, I essentially hit a block wall. In fact, I decided to shelf the idea indefinitely for as long it took to receive some inspiration. With just the title page on paper, it would certainly be the world's shortest book. As fate would have it, several weeks later I had dinner with an old friend, George Jaramillo, whom I had worked with eight years earlier. Well, when I mentioned that I was working on a book and shared the title with him, he offered to send me a poem and an essay that he had written about pain and suffering. Even though George is brilliant and one of the smartest individuals I have ever worked with, I never knew him to be a poet. In any event, he sent me his poem and essay, which are included in Chapter 2, "Inspiration". Upon reading his work, I instantly became inspired and passionate about writing. In fact, I didn't stop writing until I had completely finished.

Without even an outline of what I wanted to write about, just a title, I simply kept writing (hopefully it doesn't show through too much).

Never had I planned to write about God, but **somehow I did** and found it to be invaluable to the core message of this book. As I kept writing I quickly concluded that God is a major and absolutely indispensable key to our happiness.

I actually learned a great deal while I was writing and consolidating my collective thoughts. This "newfound knowledge" has given me increased passion for my compassion for helping others; so it was with that thought in mind that I decided to have it published even if it only motivates or helps just one person in taming their inner monkey towards their pursuit of happiness.

You are probably reading this book because I either gave it to you or a friend lent it to you; however, if you purchased it on Amazon.com, then Thank You as all of my proceeds will be used to give away more books. Since my objective is not to make money selling it, I will be giving it to as many people as I can, and in turn it is my wish that if you feel it worthy you will either lend or recommend it to others.

Last minute inclusion:

Just prior to having this book published I had an appointment with one of my doctors who was very familiar with my overall medical history and he stated that he was very impressed with my positive upbeat attitude about life. He then proceeded to explain how it was his first hand experience that those patients with a positive mental attitude fared far better than those that didn't. He then explained how patients who were told they only had two years to live and embraced a negative attitude usually died within two years, but those who embraced a positive mental attitude fared much better. As an example he told me about a lady with advanced melanoma disease that was told she only had two years to live, yet she absolutely refused to let her disease define or affect her attitude and she is still smiling and laughing eight years later and going strong. He also told me about his father who was doing very well until he was actually diagnosed and told that he had MS disease at which time he immediately shut down and became wheelchair bound. It is his belief that had his father not been told of his disease then he would not be in a wheelchair, which he attributed to his father's negative attitude towards his diagnosis. It was at that point in our conversation that I mentioned that strangely enough I had just finished writing a book that deals with mental attitudes and the power of positive thinking. I also stated that I would be giving my book away for the benefit of others, at which he informed me that doctors are always looking for ways to help their patients deal with potentially life threatening conditions and suggested that I give my book to hospital doctors. What a great idea. I immediately made that commitment, so now all I need to do is to put this plan into action, which I will be doing as soon as it is published.

God Bless

Information about the author can be read online by going to Amazon.com and entering his previous book's title: How To Succeed In Business By Really Trying / Michael Hill

Lightning Source UK Ltd.
Milton Keynes UK
UKHW010631191120
373689UK00001B/187